Material Matters

By Carrol Baker

Pearson Australia
(a division of Pearson Australia Group Pty Ltd)
707 Collins Street, Melbourne, Victoria 3008
PO Box 23360, Melbourne, Victoria 8012
www.pearson.com.au

First published 2014 by Pearson Australia
2021 2020 2019 2018
10 9 8 7 6 5 4 3 2 1

Publisher: Dian Faulisi
Project Managers: Tamara Pirois and Rachel Davis
Lead Editor: Kerry Nagle
Editor: Beth Zeme
Series & Cover Designer: Jenny Grigg
Designers: Nina Heryanto and Adam McCrow
Copyright & Pictures Editor: Katy Murenu
Mac Operator: Rob Curulli
Illustrator: Fiona Lee
Printed in Australia by the SOS Print + Media Group

ISBN 978 1 4860 0767 7
Pearson Australia Group Pty Ltd ABN 40 004 245 943

Acknowledgements
We would like to thank the following for permission to reproduce copyright material. The following abbreviations are used in this list: t = top, b = bottom, l = left, r = right, c = centre.

Corbis Australia: Roland Holschneider, p. 5.
Getty Images: Science & Society Picture Library, p. 11tr.
Shutterstock: pp. cover, 1, 3, 4, 6, 7(all), 9, 10, 11cr, 11br, 12(all), 13(all), 14, 15(all), 16(all), 17(all), 18(all), 19cr, 20, 21, 22, back cover.

Every effort has been made to trace and acknowledge copyright. However, should any infringement have occurred, the publishers tender their apologies and invite copyright owners to contact them.

Disclaimer
Some of the images used in *Material Matters* might have associations with deceased Indigenous Australians. Please be aware that these images might cause sadness or distress in Aboriginal or Torres Strait Islander communities.

Contents

A material world

The materials we touch, make and use every day are different from each other in many ways. Because materials are different, they suit different uses. What if you tried to ride a scooter made of stretchy rubber, or wear a hat made from ice blocks? Not only would you look pretty funny, your scooter and your hat wouldn't do the jobs they were meant to do!

Let's explore how and why the things we use in our world are different from each other. We'll look at the **invention** of plastic, find out why saucepans are made of metal and discover why some people live in houses made from mud.

LET'S FIND OUT

- Where do materials come from?
- What makes materials different?
- What are processed materials?
- What makes different metals and plastics useful for different **purposes**?
- Do the materials we choose affect the **environment**?

A German house made of recycled materials

Materials around us

Materials are everywhere. Think about everything around you. The grainy sand at the beach that scrunches between your toes is a material. The solid timber of your kitchen table is a material. And the smooth, clear glass on the screen of your computer is also a material.

So where do all these materials come from? Materials can be natural or processed. Natural materials are those produced by the Earth, including its plants and animals. Some natural materials are water, stone and soil. Precious metals like gold and silver are mined from the Earth and so they too are natural materials.

Processed materials are materials that humans have made by changing natural materials in some way. Processed materials include glass, rubber and plastic.

A silver nugget mined from the Earth

The properties of materials

What sets materials apart from each other? Different materials have different **properties**, or in other words they have different features.

When an object is made, the material used to make the object is considered carefully. A hair band is made of elastic because elastic is stretchy. A spoon is made of metal because metal is hard and **rigid**. A hair band made of metal would not work properly, and neither would a spoon made of elastic.

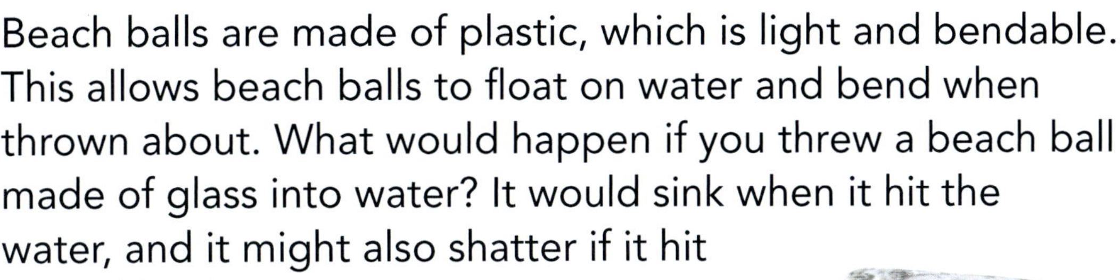

Beach balls are made of plastic, which is light and bendable. This allows beach balls to float on water and bend when thrown about. What would happen if you threw a beach ball made of glass into water? It would sink when it hit the water, and it might also shatter if it hit something hard.

Some materials have properties that can change. Water is usually a liquid that flows, but when it gets very cold, and freezes, it becomes solid, or set in its shape. So, the properties of water change when its **temperature** changes.

When water becomes very cold, it changes into ice.

In the beginning ...

Centuries ago, people had not yet learnt about all the properties of materials, or how to make processed materials, such as plastic. They had to make everything they needed out of natural materials. One popular material was stone, because it was hard and strong, and also because there was usually lots of it around. Stone was used to build shelters and weapons. Centuries later, some early stone buildings are still standing.

Timber was another popular material. It was used to make houses and boats. Peoples such as the Vikings chose to make their ships out of timber because it floats on water. If they had chosen to use a material such as stone, the ships could not have sailed.

A timber Viking ship

As people learnt more about the properties of materials, they were able to make more objects and use materials that better suited the purpose of the objects. For example, people gradually learnt that certain metals, such as iron, were very strong. And, unlike rock, these metals could also be melted and set into different shapes. This is why people began crafting tools, such as axes, from metals such as iron.

Space shuttles are built using a wide range of modern materials.

Modern materials

Today, people know how to mix natural materials and heat, cool or shape them to make new materials. These, as we have discovered, are called processed materials. Glass is an example of a processed material. It is created by mixing sand and other natural materials and heating them until they melt.

Did you know?

Graphene is a processed material that comes from the mineral graphite. It is the world's hardest known material. It is 100 times stonger than steel and only weighs 77 mg per square metre.

We use both natural and processed materials to make many large, **complex** machines as well as tiny, **intricate** gadgets. It is hard to imagine a world without plastic toys, PlayStations® or cars.

Fantastic plastic

There are two main types of plastics: thermosets (which are rigid and keep their shape unless heated to very high temperatures) and thermoplastics (which are softer and can be melted at lower temperatures). Some of the natural materials used to make plastic are crude oil and coal.

Plastic is a popular material because it has many useful properties: it is **mouldable**, waterproof, hard wearing, easy to clean and cheap to buy. We use objects made from plastics every day. Plastics are used to produce toothbrushes, buttons, computer keyboards and lunchboxes.

Plastic buttons

The invention of plastic

The very first type of plastic was invented by Alexander Parkes in 1856 while he was trying to create a **replica** of ivory (which comes from elephant tusks). The type of plastic he invented came to be known as celluloid.

Portrait of Alexander Parkes

Several years later, John Hyatt entered a competition to create a replacement for ivory in billiard balls. Hyatt improved celluloid so that it was stronger and more stable, as well as cheaper and simpler to create. Soon, billiard balls were made from Hyatt's celluloid. And not long after it was also used in the film on which movies were shot!

More toys!

Plastic has changed the world of toy making. Before plastic came along, most toys were made by hand from wood, metal or cloth. Now, machines create plastic toys by shaping heated plastic to **moulds**. This method is cheap and allows many toys to be created quickly. Plastic is used to make toys such as building blocks, hula hoops, skateboard wheels and many more!

Plastic hearts

Plastic isn't only used to make toys. It is also used to save lives. Scientists have used plastic to make a range of **artificial** body parts, including artificial hearts. Artificial hearts have pumps that act like the right and left **ventricles** of a regular heart. They can pump up to 9.5 litres of blood through the body per minute.

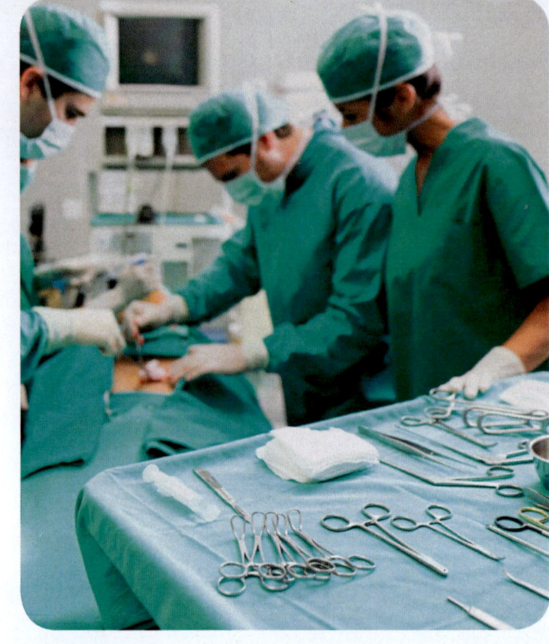

Artificial hearts are placed during surgery

Doctors began developing artificial hearts in the 1960s and the technology has improved a great deal since then. In 2010, a Sydney man, Angelo Tigano, received the Southern Hemisphere's first total artificial heart implant.

It's a wrap

School lunches are often covered in plastic wrap to keep them fresh. Cling wrap was discovered in 1933 by Ralph Wiley, an American chemical lab worker. He was trying to clean the remains of an experiment out of a container, but the remains were stuck to the edges. This became the first type of plastic wrap. To begin with, it was used to cover aircraft, to protect them from salt air spray. It was only later that it was used to keep food fresh.

Today, cling wrap is made in factories using large machinery. Polyethylene (a type of plastic) is created from crude oil and then heated to 200–300 degrees Celsius. Once melted, air is blown through the hot plastic, causing it to form what looks like a large bubble. This thin bubble of plastic is then flattened and wound on to a roller. Before being sent out to shops, the cling wrap is tested to ensure that it is strong, sticky and stretchy; it must be able to stretch to seven times its original length to pass the test!

Stronger types of cling wrap are available, which can hold cartons together and protect them from moisture.

Cling wrap stretches around food to seal it and keep it fresh.

Did you know?

Australia was the first country in the world to have a system of bank notes made from a plastic called polypropylene. Plastic bank notes are more difficult to replicate than paper notes. They also last four times longer and are more **hygienic**.

Heavy metal

Most of the centre of our planet is made of metal. The solid inner core and the liquid outer core are made up mainly of iron and nickel, which are both metals. Metal can also be found in the Earth's surface. We take some of these metals out of the Earth to make tools, utensils, jewellery, building materials, cars and even bridges. Metals are used to make these objects and structures because most metals are hard and strong.

Shaping metal

Some well-known metals are iron, gold, silver and tin. These metals can be bent into all sorts of shapes using different processes. One process is called casting, and is similar to making jelly in a mould. The hot **molten** metal is poured into a mould, and then cools and hardens into the shape of the mould. Many car parts are made like this, as well as metal beams for constructing buildings and objects such as taps. There are several methods of casting. One is called die-casting; in this method, the molten metal is injected into the mould through a small hole.

Molten metal being poured into a mould

Aluminium cans are made using a process called machining. This is where the aluminium is flattened into sheets and then cut by a machine into the correct shape. On its own, aluminium is not very useful, because it is quite soft. However, it does have many useful properties; for example, it is light in weight and does not rust easily. Aluminium is often mixed with other harder metals, such as zinc and silicon for use in objects such as car parts.

When metals are mixed together, the resulting material is called an alloy. Alloys are created to make a stronger, more **durable** material. Silver and copper can be mixed together to create an alloy. This alloy is used in doctors' medical instruments and in musical instruments. Steel is also an alloy – a mixture of iron, carbon and other elements. Steel is cast, or melted into moulds, to make steel beams for buildings.

Rusty metals

Over time, some metals begin to rust or **corrode**, and get eaten away. This happens when oxygen reacts with a metal. These metals can be painted to prevent oxygen from reaching the metal's surface and causing it to corrode. The metals can also be coated with another metal that does not corrode, such as zinc.

The metal on this car would have corroded over time.

Dig it!

Sometimes metals can be found quite easily on the Earth's surface. However, metal is often deeper in the Earth's surface and needs to be dug out, using a method called mining.

Metals are mostly found in ore, which is rock that contains minerals such as metals. The ore itself is mined and then the metal is separated out of the ore. One method of separation is called smelting. This is where the metal is heated until it melts, filtering out the unmelted ore. Chemicals that combine with the non-metal ore are also used, drawing them out and separating them from the metal.

Did you know?

Most metals are solid unless they are heated to a high temperature. There is one type of metal, though, that is liquid at average room temperature, which is called mercury.

Mining underground for ore

Metal conductors

Metals are very good **conductors** of heat, meaning that they absorb and transfer heat easily. This is the reason we make items such as saucepans out of metal.

When a saucepan heats up, it cooks the food inside without melting. The saucepan would have to be heated to extreme temperatures in order for it to melt. Steel, for example, melts at around 1370 degrees Celsius.

Metals are also good conductors of electricity, meaning they can carry an electrical current. This is why metal wires are used to carry electricity.

This metal saucepan will heat quickly and cook the food inside.

Precious metals

Centuries ago, the Romans, among other peoples, melted valuable metals such as gold and silver to make coins. Now cheaper metals, such as copper and nickel, are used.

Australian coins are today made mainly of copper and nickel.

Build it

Imagine living in a house made of ice? What about a cosy cottage made from mud? These days, many modern homes are built from bricks or wood, but there are many different types of building materials.

Early homes

People a long time ago did not have the option of using processed materials to build their homes. But they still had to choose materials that had the right properties. Some early shelters were made using animal skins, which are tough and hard wearing. Another early building material was stone, which is also hard and sturdy.

Mud houses

Yes, it's true – houses can be made from mud! Mud, clay and water can be mixed together and shaped into bricks. When the mud bricks dry out, they become hard. Mud bricks keep out the cold and keep the heat in – so you stay toasty warm in winter and cool in summer.

Mud bricks

Long ago, many people built houses out of mud bricks because mud was easy to find and use. Later, people began to use stronger, processed materials. Today, though, mud bricks are becoming a popular building material again! One reason for this is that mud bricks are environmentally friendly. They are made from natural materials without harmful chemicals.

Ice houses

Imagine living in an ice house! The Inuit in the Arctic lived in ice igloos. You may think that a house made of ice would be a very cold place to live but, actually, ice houses did keep the Inuit warm. The igloos often had a fire burning inside them, and the ice bricks kept the warm air inside. The hard blocks of ice were built in a spiral form, making a very strong structure. A hole in the roof let out smoke and a tunnel led to the outside. The igloos were quite bare inside, but often there was an ice brick bed to sleep on!

An igloo – a type of house made of ice

Concrete towers

Modern buildings can be many storeys high. These tall buildings, often called skyscrapers, are made from concrete. Concrete is made by mixing sand, gravel, water and cement. It is poured into moulds to shape it and sets very hard. Concrete is hard wearing and can be made into large sheets, allowing buildings to be made quickly. Tall buildings made from concrete are reinforced with steel poles to make the buildings even stronger. This is particularly important in buildings constructed in areas where earthquakes occur.

The tallest building in the world today is Burj Khalifa in Dubai. It is 828 metres high – almost one kilometre! Burj Khalifa was constructed using 330 000 cubic metres of concrete and took about 22 million hours to complete.

The Burj Khalifa building, Dubai

A traditional-style Japanese house

Paper houses

Traditional Japanese houses were built from paper, wood, straw and bamboo. Thick rice paper was wrapped around timber frames for the walls, which allowed breeze and light to enter the houses. Some walls were actually sliding doors, also made of wood and paper, that could open or close to change room sizes.

Did you know?

The Chocolate Mill, a chocolate factory in Victoria, is made from straw. The Wat Pa Maha Chedi Kaew temple in Thailand is made from one million glass beer bottles. In Bolivia, the Palacio de Sal is a hotel made entirely of salt blocks.

Connections

We live on an amazing planet. Many useful materials can be found in our natural environment and we are able to create a good many others.

Some materials have a greater effect on the environment than others. Materials that have a low impact on the environment are described as **sustainable**. Bamboo is a sustainable material because it grows naturally and breaks down naturally to become part of the Earth again.

Plastic bags are not considered sustainable. They are produced using chemicals and do not break down easily. They have been designed to be durable and so they float around our environment for many years before breaking down.

As well as choosing materials that do not harm the environment, it is important that we consider the amount of materials we use, as there are only limited amounts of many of them. It is our responsibility to think about how many 'things' we need and which ones we can recycle or re-use.

Glossary

artificial not real; human-made copy

complex having lots of different parts

conductors allow something (such as heat or electricity) to pass through

corrode eat away

durable hard wearing; long lasting

environment surroundings

hygienic clean; protects from disease

intricate detailed; complex

invention something new or unique

molten in a liquid state due to heat

mouldable its shape can be changed

moulds hollowed shapes that can be filled to create objects of that shape

properties special qualities or features

purposes reasons for use

replica a copy of something else

rigid stiff, not moveable

sustainable can be continued because it does little harm to the environment or does not use up Earth's resources

temperature the level of heat

ventricles hollow spaces in the heart that hold and pump blood

Index